W9-BYR-536

Dedicated to Callum, Ben, Sonora, Quinn
and little ballers everywhere.

Copyright © 2018 by James Littlejohn and Matthew Shipley

No part of this publication may be reproduced, stored in a retrieval system, or transmitted in any form by any means, electronic, mechanical, photocopying, or otherwise, without the prior written permission of the publisher, Triumph Books LLC, 814 North Franklin Street, Chicago, Illinois 60610.

Library of Congress Cataloging-in-Publication Data available upon request.

This book is available in quantity at special discounts for your group or organization. For further information, contact:
Triumph Books LLC
814 North Franklin Street
Chicago, Illinois 60610
(312) 337-0747
www.triumphbooks.com

Printed in China
ISBN: 978-1-62937-588-5

A IS FOR AIR

The Wright Brothers invented flight.
Michael "Air" Jordan perfected it.

B IS FOR BIRD

The legendary Larry Bird chirped with the best of them, but he had the game to back it up.

C IS FOR COOKING

If you can't stand the heat, stay out of the kitchen – the Beard is cooking.

D IS FOR DOCTOR

His game was clinical.
His operating room an arena.
The one and only Dr. J.

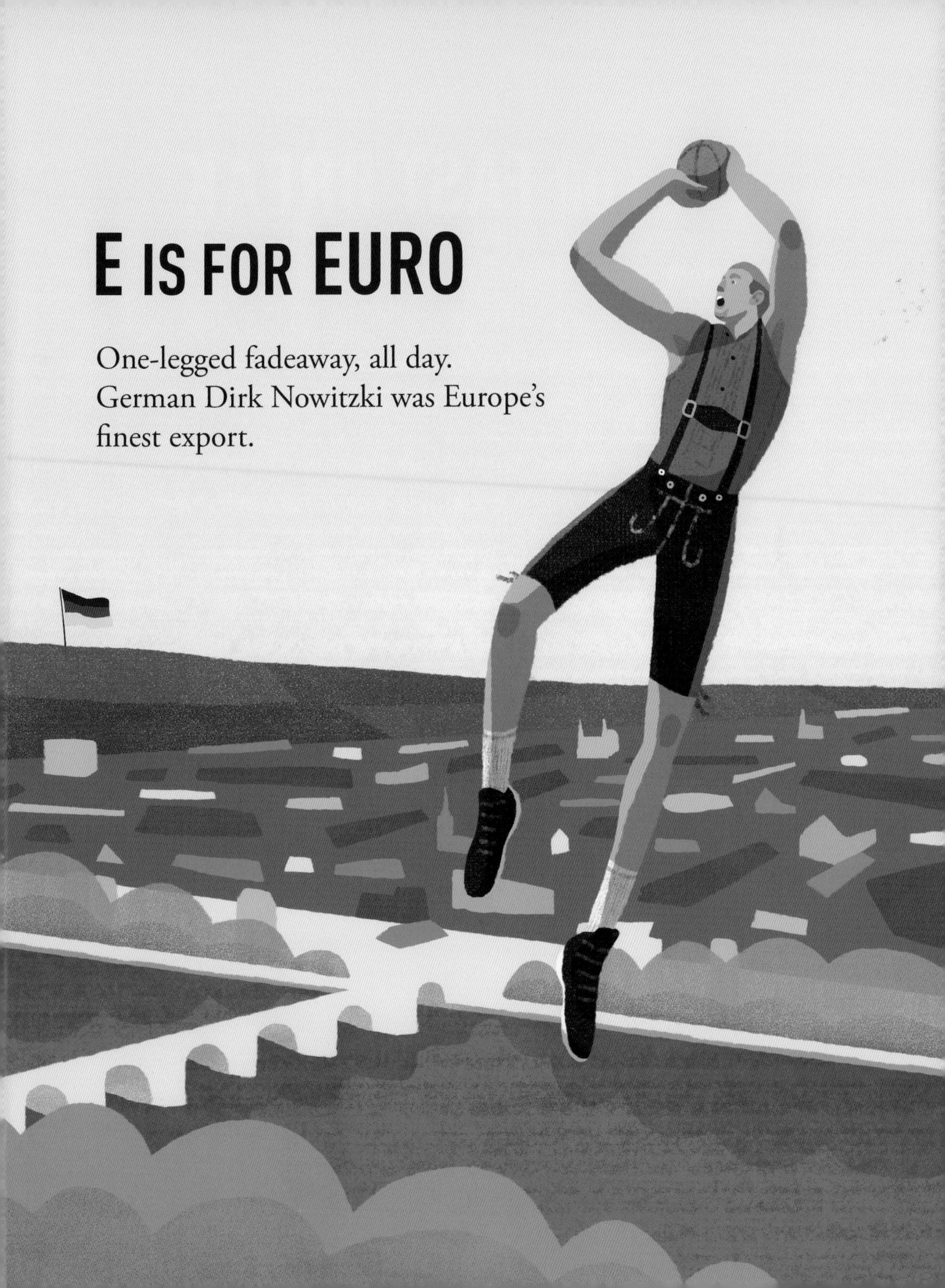

E IS FOR EURO

One-legged fadeaway, all day. German Dirk Nowitzki was Europe's finest export.

F IS FOR FAST BREAK

Two-time MVP Steve Nash could burn your defense in seven seconds or less.

G IS FOR GRANDMAMA

Sorry Madea, "Grandmama" Larry Johnson is the real G-GOAT – the Greatest Grandma of All Time.

H IS FOR HUGE HUMAN HURTING HOOPS

Bring it down, big fella, bring it down. Shaq's super strength left a pile of broken backboards in his path.

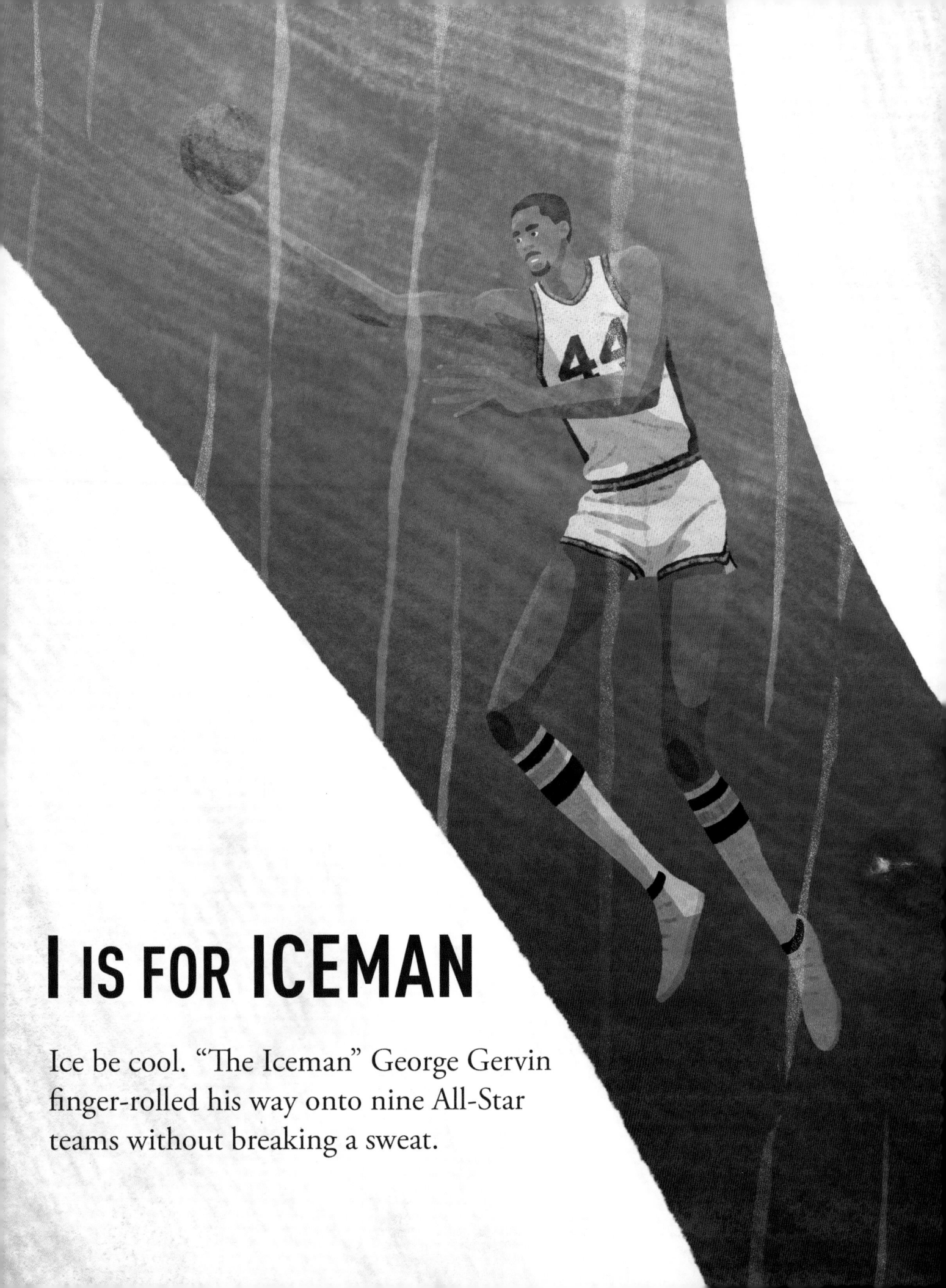

I IS FOR ICEMAN

Ice be cool. "The Iceman" George Gervin finger-rolled his way onto nine All-Star teams without breaking a sweat.

J IS FOR JAM

Jam on. When Bill Walton wasn't jamming on the court, he was jamming with the Grateful Dead.

K IS FOR KING

Pass, board, score or defend. They call him the King because LeBron can do it all.

L IS FOR LITTLE

Just 5-foot-3, little Muggsy Bogues lasted fourteen seasons in the land of giants.

M IS FOR MAILMAN

High on the mountain top, a postman's on patrol. Watch out – when Karl sets a pick, it's hard to slow the roll.

N IS FOR NINETIES

What a time to be alive.

33
34
THE GLOVE
REIGN MAN
STOCKTON
PIP
SIR CHARLES

O IS FOR ONE HUNDRED

Only one man ever scored one hundred points in one game: Wilt Chamberlain.

P IS FOR PISTOL

"Pistol" Pete averaged 44 points a game in college. If they had threes back then, he'd have averaged over 50.

Q IS FOR QUESTION

And the ANSWER is ALLEN IVERSON
– 165 pounds of pure heart.

R IS FOR RINGS

Quiet and consistent, Tim Duncan knew a thing or ~~two~~ five about winning: It don't mean a thing without that ring.

2
MAGIC

S IS FOR SHOWTIME

Pull up a seat. Enjoy the show. Magic and crew are putting on a performance.

CURRY
30

T IS FOR THREES

Layups are nice and dunks are dope,
but threes are better 'cause they're worth the most.

U IS FOR UNCLE

Listen up, youngbloods: Uncle Drew and his buddy Bill Russell need you to understand that this game has always been, and will always be, about buckets.

V IS FOR VENOM

Beware. Kobe was known to strike like the venomous Black Mamba – the fastest, most feared snake in the world.

W IS FOR WORM

Wriggling, wrestling and worming for every board, Dennis Rodman wasn't afraid to do the dirty work down low.

X IS FOR X'S AND O'S
They know their X's. They know their O's. Coaches change the game without ever touching the rock.
POP

Y IS FOR YOU THE REAL MVP

His arms are slender. His heart is tender. It doesn't matter what he says, KD is the real MVP.

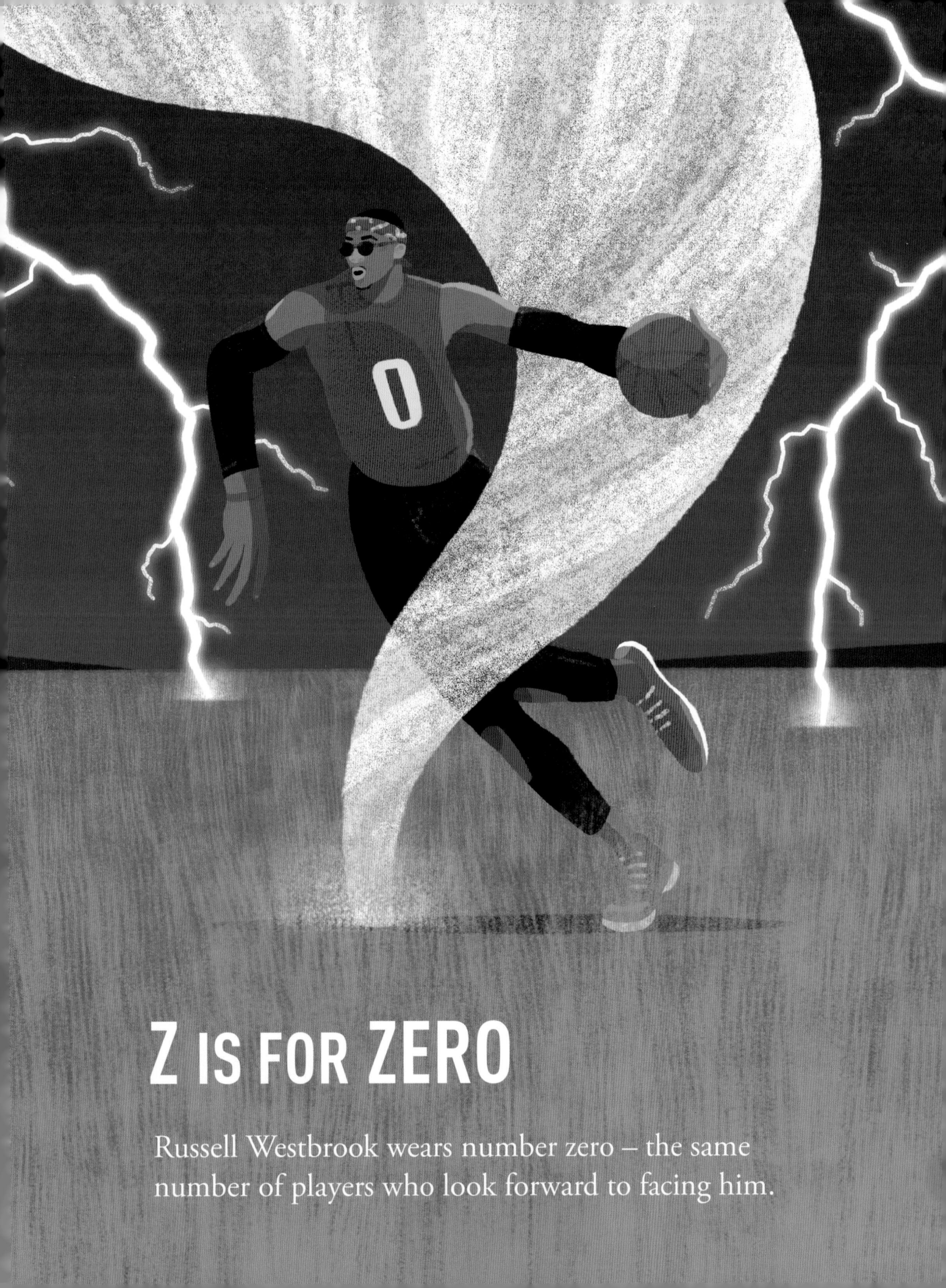

Z IS FOR ZERO

Russell Westbrook wears number zero – the same number of players who look forward to facing him.